W9-CDE-733

POLAR BEARS

A TRUE BOOK®

by
Ann O. Squire

Children's Press®
A Division of Scholastic Inc.

New York Toronto London Auckland Sydney
Mexico City New Delhi Hong Kong
Danbury, Connecticut

A scientist placing a tracking collar on a sedated polar bear

Content Consultant
Kathy Carlstead, PhD
*Research Scientist
Honolulu Zoo*

Reading Consultant
Cecilia Minden-Cupp, PhD
*Former Director, Language
and Literacy Program
Harvard Graduate School
of Education*

Author's Dedication
For Emma and Evan

*The photographs on the cover
and title page show polar
bears in the Arctic.*

Library of Congress Cataloging-in-Publication Data
Squire, Ann.
    Polar bears / by Ann O. Squire.
       p. cm. — (A True Book)
    Includes bibliographical references and index.
    ISBN-10: 0-516-25473-1 (lib. bdg.)   0-516-25584-3 (pbk.)
    ISBN-13: 978-0-516-25473-9 (lib. bdg.)   978-0-516-25584-2 (pbk.)
    1. Polar bear—Juvenile literature. I. Title. II. Series.
QL737.C27S66 2006
599.786—dc22   2005003636

CHILDREN'S PRESS, and A TRUE BOOK™, and associated logos are
trademarks and/or registered trademarks of Scholastic Library Publishing.
SCHOLASTIC and associated logos are trademarks and/or registered
trademarks of Scholastic Inc.
1 2 3 4 5 6 7 8 9 10 R 16 15 14 13 12 11 10 09 08 07

Contents

A polar bear walks on Arctic land.

Bears of the Frozen North

When you think of the Arctic's treeless, snowy land and drifting ice, it's impossible not to think of the polar bear. Everything about the Arctic makes you think of this big white bear.

The word *Arctic* comes from *arktikos*, the ancient Greek

word for "country of the great bear." You might wonder how the Greeks, who had never seen a polar bear, came up with this name. They named the region after the group of stars in the northern sky called Ursa Major, which means "great bear."

The polar bear is the Arctic's top **predator**. That means there is no larger Arctic animal that hunts other animals for food. In fact, the

The world's largest land predator is the polar bear.

polar bear is the largest land predator in the world.

Weighing up to 1,500 pounds (680 kilograms), a male polar bear is more than twice as big as a Siberian tiger. Female polar bears are less than half that size. They weigh up to about 660 pounds (300 kg).

Polar bears live in the northern reaches of Alaska, Canada, Russia, Norway, and Greenland. They travel long distances over the sea ice in search of seals.

It might be surprising to learn that a Siberian tiger (top) is less than half the size of a male polar bear (bottom).

A polar bear in Norway moves across the sea ice on a hunt for seals.

Seals are their favorite food.
When seals are plentiful, a
polar bear doesn't have to go

far to find something to eat. The bear's home range can be as small as a few hundred square miles.

A bear must search a much bigger area when seals are hard to find. One female polar bear surprised scientists by walking and swimming from Alaska to Greenland, on to Canada, and back to Greenland again. The total distance she covered was nearly 3,000 miles (4,828 kilometers)!

At Home in the Water

Polar bears are skillful swimmers. These huge animals can travel in the water for hours when moving from one chunk of sea ice to another. The polar bear is built for swimming. Its long neck keeps the bear's head above water. Its huge webbed feet serve as paddles in the water. The coat of the polar bear repels water.

A swimming polar bear

Subzero Survival

Scientists believe that polar bears changed slowly over time, or **evolved**, from brown bears beginning about 100,000 years ago. As they became more and more different from brown bears, they also became better suited to life in the North's bitter cold.

Winter in the high Arctic is dark. The sun sets in October and doesn't rise again until February. It is also very cold. The average temperature in January and February is −29 degrees Fahrenheit (−34 degrees Celsius).

The polar bear's body has changed, or **adapted**, to survive these extreme conditions. The polar bear has a thick layer of fat under its fur called **blubber**. The blubber is more

Blubber, a thick layer of fat under the fur, helps keep the polar bear warm.

than 4 inches (10 centimeters) thick and protects the bear's body against the cold.

The fur of a polar bear has two layers. The first layer is a fuzzy undercoat. This layer traps warm air near the polar bear's body.

The second layer of fur has guard hairs that repel water. The guard hairs appear to be white. In fact, these hairs are clear. The polar bear's fur just looks white because of the way it reflects light. Except for its black nose and the bottoms

Polar bear fur has an outside layer of hairs that repels water.

of its feet, the polar bear is covered with fur from head to toe.

The huge polar bear has small ears and a short tail.

The polar bear's ears and tail are very small. They are much smaller than those of other bears. The polar bear's body has adapted to the cold. The bear loses heat quickly from these areas, so small ears and a short tail help the animal keep warm.

The polar bear adapts to the cold in other ways as well. During fierce winter storms, a bear often digs a shelter in a snowbank. Then the bear curls

A polar bear warms its nose with its paw.

up with its back to the wind to wait out the bad weather. The bear sometimes uses its furry paw to keep its nose warm.

With all these special features, it's easy to see how polar bears survive the Arctic winter. But what do they do when summer comes? Bears can't take off their heavy winter coats like people can. In the summer, polar bears rest when they can and walk instead of run to keep from overheating.

The Seal Hunters

Polar bears hunt ringed seals. They travel over the Arctic ice looking for these animals. Polar bears walk on the ice in both summer and winter.

Walking on ice is slippery and dangerous for humans. But polar bears have adapted in some ways that make it easy.

A polar bear and her cub hunt for seals on the ice during the summer.

Tiny bumps on the paw, long claws, and fur between the toes keep the polar bear from slipping on the ice.

First, their paws are huge. They are up to 12 inches (30 cm) wide. The large surface of the paw helps to spread out the body weight when the polar bear walks on thin ice.

Second, the bottoms of the paws are covered with tiny bumps called **papillae**. These bumps grip the ice and keep the bear from slipping. Long, curved claws and tufts of fur between the toes also help steady the bear on the ice.

In the summer, the polar bear hunts seals that are resting or sleeping on the ice. The bear creeps toward the sleeping seal, stopping if the seal wakes and raises its head. It can be hard to see the white polar bear against the white snow and ice. From about 20 feet (6 meters) away, the bear pounces and kills the seal before it can slip back into the water.

In the winter, seals spend their time underneath the thick Arctic ice. Because they are **mammals**, they must breathe air. So each seal cuts ten to fifteen breathing holes in the ice before winter

A polar bear captures a seal.

arrives. The seal pops up through one of the holes to take a breath every five to fifteen minutes. The seal keeps these holes open all winter long, even when the ice is 6 feet (1.8 m) thick.

A hungry polar bear uses its powerful sense of smell to find a breathing hole, then settles down to wait. The bear knows that a seal must use the breathing hole. Because seals use many different holes, the bear's wait can be long. The polar bear is patient. When a seal finally surfaces for air, the polar bear grabs it with its sharp claws and drags it out of the water.

Two polar bears wait on the ice for seals to surface (top). A seal pops up through a breathing hole (bottom).

Mothers and Cubs

A female polar bear usually has her first cubs when she is five or six years old. In the spring, the bear looks around for a mate. After mating, she spends the summer hunting, eating, and packing on as much fat as possible. A female bear may gain nearly

After mating, the female polar bear digs a hole in a snowdrift as protection against the cold.

450 pounds (204 kg) as she prepares to have her cubs.

In the fall, the female digs a den in a snowdrift. A short tunnel connects the den to the outside. Another hole in the ceiling provides fresh air. Her body heat and the packed snow keep the pregnant bear snug and warm in her small den.

In the winter, the female gives birth to one or two cubs. The newborn bears are only about 12 inches (30 cm) long. They weigh only about 1 pound (0.45 kg). Their eyes are closed, and they are covered with fine fur.

A mother bear and her cub peer out from their den.

The cubs stay close to their mother for warmth. Their eyes open within the first month. By two months, they are learning to walk inside the den. It is too cold for them to venture outside.

The cubs drink their mother's rich milk to survive. The mother bear does not eat at all. She fed heavily before entering the den. She will not eat again until the cubs are ready to emerge from the den.

In the spring, the mother bear leads her cubs out of the den for the first time. They now weigh between 20 and 30 pounds (9 and 14 kg). After a little practice outdoors, they can walk and run easily.

Two polar bear cubs drink their mother's milk.

The mother soon travels with her cubs to the sea ice to hunt. When she catches a seal, the cubs get their first taste of solid food. The little bears grow quickly on their mother's milk and on the seals she catches.

The cubs learn to hunt by watching their mother. But hunting takes practice. It may be nearly two years before the cubs can capture a seal on their own.

When they are between two and three years old, the young bears have learned how to survive in the wild. Now the mother bear is ready to breed again. She

A mother bear leads her cubs across the ice.

chases her cubs away. It is time for them to begin life on their own.

Polar Bears in Danger

People in the Arctic have always hunted polar bears. They ate the meat and used the skins for clothing. Hunting was the biggest danger for polar bears for many years. Now that there are laws protecting polar bears in the wild, hunting in most places is not the danger it once was.

A polar bear in Canada investigates a bear trap.

Global warming means earlier spring thaws and less time for polar bears to walk and hunt on the Arctic ice.

Polar bears remain in trouble, however. **Global warming**, the gradual warming of Earth's climate, threatens them.

Polar bears must travel over sea ice to hunt seals. As Earth's climate gets warmer, Arctic ice is melting earlier each spring. More ice is melting, too. Melting shortens the time polar bears can hunt. It also reduces the amount of ice they can hunt on.

The result is that polar bears aren't eating as many seals. Today's polar bears are smaller and have fewer cubs than in the past.

Another problem for polar bears is pollution of the Arctic. Chemicals in the oceans end up in the fat of seals that polar bears eat. These poisons make the bears sick and lower the number of healthy polar bear cubs.

Reducing pollution of the Arctic and managing changes in the world's climate are big jobs. These challenges must be met if we are to save polar bears and the unspoiled Arctic wilderness in which they live.

A mother polar bear and her cub stand on an iceberg.

To Find Out More

Here are some additional resources to help you learn more about polar bears:

 **Books**

Canizares, Susan, and Daniel Moreton. **Polar Bears = Osos Polares**. Scholastic, 2002.

Lockwood, Sophie. **Polar Bears**. Child's World, 2005.

Ovsyanikov, Nikita. **Polar Bears**. Voyageur Press, 2002.

Patent, Dorothy Hinshaw. **Polar Bears**. Lerner Publishing, 2000.

Ryder, Joanne. **A Pair of Polar Bears: Twin Cubs Find a Home at the San Diego Zoo**. Simon & Schuster Books for Young Readers, 2006.

Sjonger, Rebecca, and Bobbie Kalman. **The Life Cycle of a Polar Bear**. Crabtree Publishing, 2005.

☀ Organizations and Online Sites

Alaska Zoo
4731 O'Malley Road
Anchorage, AK 99507
907-346-2133
*http://www.alaskazoo.org/
index.htm*

The Alaska Zoo is home to almost 100 birds and mammals, including a polar bear. Click on the "Virtual Tour" button to see an illustrated map of the zoo with links.

Defenders of Wildlife
1130 17th Street NW
Washington, DC 20036
800-385-9712
*http://www.defenders.org/
wildlife/new/polarbears.html*

Look for information about environmental threats to polar bears as well as a polar bear fact sheet and video clip.

Polar Bears International
PO Box 66142
Baton Rouge, LA 70806
225-923-3114
*http://www.polarbears
international.org*

Learn more about protecting the polar bear, view photo galleries and webcam photos of polar bears, and check out a worldwide list of zoos with polar bears.

Polar Bears, National Geographic Kids
*http://www.national
geographic.com/kids/creature
_feature/0004/polar.html*

The site offers polar bear fun facts, video and audio clips, and postcards.

World Wildlife Fund
1250 24th Street NW
Washington, DC 20037
202-293-4800
*http://www.worldwildlife.org
/polarbears/index.cfm*

Learn more about wildlife conservation and polar bears around the world and read the field notes of a scientist tracking polar bears in Canada.

45

Important Words

adapt to change in order to survive better

blubber a thick layer of fat under the skin of polar bears and other sea mammals

evolve to change slowly over time

global warming gradual warming of Earth's climate

mammals warm-blooded animals that breathe air and nurse their young

papillae tiny bumps on a polar bear's foot pads that grip the ice and keep the bear from slipping

predator an animal that hunts and eats other animals

Index

Meet the Author

Ann O. Squire has a PhD in animal behavior. Before becoming a writer, she spent several years studying African electric fish and the special signals they use to communicate with each other. Dr. Squire is the author of many books on natural science and animals, including *Beluga Whales, Lemmings, Moose, Penguins,* and *Puffins*. She lives with her family in Katonah, New York.